On the Side of the Angels

by Jose Amaujaq Kusugak

Illustrated by Hwei Lim

QINUISAARNIQ Qinuisaarniq ("resiliency") is a program created to educate Nunavummiut and all Canadians about the history and impacts of residential schools, policies of assimilation, and other colonial acts that affected the Canadian Arctic.

Published in Canada by Inhabit Education Books Inc. | www.inhabiteducation.com

Inhabit Education Books Inc.
(Iqaluit) P.O. Box 2129, Iqaluit, Nunavut, X0A 1H0
(Toronto) 191 Eglinton Avenue East, Suite 301, Toronto, Ontario, M4P 1K1

This memoir originally appeared in *Response, Responsibility, and Renewal: Canada's Truth and Reconciliation Journey*, published in 2009 by the Aboriginal Healing Foundation.

Printed in Canada.

Library and Archives Canada Cataloguing in Publication

Title: On the side of the angels / by Jose Amaujaq Kusugak ; illustrated by Hwei Lim.
Other titles: Contained in (work): Response, responsibility and renewal.
Names: Kusugak, Jose, 1950-2011. | Lim, Hwei, 1980- illustrator.
Description: Previously published as a chapter in: Response, responsibility and renewal : Canada's truth and reconciliation journey / edited for the Aboriginal Healing Foundation by Gregory Younging, Jonathan Dewar, Mike DeGagné. Ottawa : Aboriginal Healing Foundation, 2009.
Identifiers: Canadiana 20190177683 | ISBN 9781774502037 (softcover)
Subjects: LCSH: Kusugak, Jose, 1950-2011. | LCSH: Kusugak, Jose, 1950-2011—Childhood and youth. |
LCSH: Off-reservation boarding schools—Canada—History. | LCSH: Inuit—Abuse of—Canada—History. |
LCSH: Inuit—Education—Canada—History. | LCSH: Inuit—Canada—Social conditions. | LCSH: Inuit—Cultural assimilation—Canada. | LCSH: Inuit—Canada—Biography. | CSH: Inuit—Canada—Residential schools.
Classification: LCC E99.E7 K87 2020 | DDC 371.829/9712071—dc23

ISBN: 978-1-77450-203-7

INHABIT EDUCATION BOOKS

Content Note

This book deals with subject matter that may be difficult for readers, including descriptions of sexual abuse.

Health Canada help line: 1-866-925-4419
Nunavut Kamatsiaqtut help line: 1-867-979-3333 / 1-800-265-3333

Contents

The Bay

The Hudson's Bay Company (HBC), or "The Bay," was incorporated on May 2, 1670, making it the oldest incorporated company in the world. Two hundred and eighty years later, on May 2, 1950, I was born into the "Bay" in Naujaat (Repulse Bay), where my mother and father both worked for the HBC. On my birthdays, the trader would point to the HBC insignia on their main store and give me a present, which was often a sucker candy. I would slurp it with pride to make all around me jealous with envy. The HBC, with all its own problems, was not in the Arctic to change Inuit people. It was there because of the furs it wanted to obtain from Inuit hunters, who were master hunters of Arctic animals.

Healthy hunters brought in more furs, so the HBC gave their traders minimal training on meeting the medical needs of Inuit hunters. I have even seen them pulling teeth and giving shots when necessary. Inuit and "The Bay" had a good partnership. Inuit wanted the goods, and The Bay wanted the furs. The Bay boys learned Inuktitut, the language of Inuit, so there was very little assimilation of Inuit toward the *Qallunaaq* (white people) world. Qallunaaq HBC boys wrote several books praising Inuit knowledge, culture, and perseverance. This was not from the goodness of their hearts necessarily; it was but an acknowledgement of what the HBC employees needed and wanted to learn from Inuit on Arctic survival.

Even the churches, who were appalled at the shamanistic rituals of Inuit in some regions, only wanted to save souls and not necessarily change culture. They were not necessarily anti-Inuit, but were just not Inuit. Many Inuit became Christians because the churches had what Inuit wanted: biscuits, beans, prunes, hope, and gifts of clothing from other Christians in the south. I remember there was always a strong smell of mothballs in the clothing, which is one of the first Qallunaaq smells we encountered.

My mother did not like the HBC's practice of stockpiling the furs of bear, fox, seal, and other fur commodities throughout the winter. But in the spring, at the first sign of break-up of the creeks and rivers, she would then start cleaning the furs with Sunlight soap, brisk floor brush, ulu, and flour. She would do this work until the ship came in to collect her pressed and sewn bales of fur.

An Arctic Childhood

Life as children at that time was pretty carefree. For all we knew, there were at least two kinds of Qallunaat in this world: traders and priests. There would be an occasional airplane that came in to bring groceries and magazines. When the traders were done with the magazines, they would give them to my mother, and she would then redo the wallpaper in our *qarmaq* (sod house) with new pictures from the magazines and a flour-and-water paste. Sometimes, lemmings would be just on the other side of the wallpaper, eating the flour. (When someone needed boils and other skin ailments tended to, my father would sometimes harvest lemmings and use them as gauzes.) A capital *H* is shaped like *aqsaaraq*, an Inuit finger-pulling game of strength. So my siblings and I would play *aqsaaraqtaaqpunga*, a game of finding capital *H*'s in the magazine text on the walls. When we got tired of aqsaaraqtaaqpunga, we would play *nimiriaqtaaqpunga*, or finding capital *S*'s, because they were shaped like snakes or worms.

As Roman Catholics, we would go to catechism, where we were taught about the "earth maker," Nunaliuqti (God), who was the Almighty. We were taught that when His son comes down from heaven to gather believers, the ones going to heaven would go to his right side, and the ones going to hell would go to his left side. It dawned on me one day that the HBC side of Naujaat would be on the left side of Jesus when he descends into the sea, so my younger brother Cyril and I used to practise running to the church side so we would be ready when His son does come down.

After one of these exercises, we came into the qarmaq, where my mother was re-wallpapering and my father was skinning foxes and smoking his corncob pipe. Mother asked why we were out of breath, and after I explained, she asked Father to tell us "the truth." Father stood up slowly with his bloodied hands and messed-up long hair, and, with a drag from his pipe, he made a halo shape with his hair around his head. With his hands to his side dripping blood, he looked like Jesus Christ himself, and he said, "My sons, Jesus would come down from the land side, which would put us on the right hand of God." Mother mumbled something like, "Husband!" but that was a good enough answer for me and Cyril, and off we went, knowing we were safe.

We were all taught from birth our roles in life on this world. Boys were promised to girls sometimes at birth; their relationship to each other depended on their given names. Rules of life were taught, and this was communicated orally, since Inuit had no written language—history, folklore, sciences, music, rites of passage, and so on. During hardships of any kind, great care was given to having at least one survivor pass on the history. Just like the Qallunaat, Inuit had hypotheses and did experiments to get to the scientific conclusion. As they could not write the conclusion down, for memory they would make it into a taboo, like, "If you do not follow it you will die within a year." Sometimes messages were given in pictographs, but mostly they depicted the environment, like weather, ice conditions, the fatness of caribou, husky dog behaviour, seasons, and wind directions. Anything to do with the necessities of life, we were taught to read through pictographs.

Since Inuit have an oral history and communication, lying was a "deadly sin," because it could lead to the death of someone. The number-one commandment was, "Obey your father and mother and your uncles and aunts without verifiable evidence, but understand everyone and anyone else could be lying to you." The number-two commandment was, "Respect the environment, for you are a part of it." Inuit look at themselves as part of the ecosystem.

This is not to say that Inuit were a perfect race; they were not. Society control was harsh. Most people were paired off as *iviriit*, or "ratters," to each other. If Inuit found you cheating, stealing, or doing unmentionables, they did not approach you directly; instead, they would tell your *iviq*, your "ratter." Your ratter would wait until there was a large gathering, and then put your "sins" to music and publicize your sins that way. It was a real shame to be put into a song publicly.

Inuit were socialists but kept their own implements. They could ante their things when gambling, but had to share their harvest of animals, to the point that it was possible for a successful hunter not to get anything from his hunt, which would be a source of pride for the hunter. Until the hunter shared his harvest, his cache of meat would be stored, but it was never to be disturbed by someone else, even when found by people who were starving. This was not a law, but the people had such pride in respecting other people's "things" that they would rather starve. This did not include everyone, of course, but most people.

The whole basis of learning was through observation and through bettering what had been observed while respecting the environment. We were taught the neuroplasticity of the brain: the use of the brain is infinite. Our brains can communicate with spirits. We can transcend to check on our relatives' situation by meditating. We can become shamans by befriending spirits. This was not a religion, but a science of the brain that was achievable. The spirit world, being real of course, also had its own rules, and shamans had to follow and obey them. These are known as *tirigusungniq*, or "not to hurt or break the rules of the spirits." Inuit Christians followed these rules and knew they were not breaking the commandments of the Holy Bible. Commandment number one says, "Do not serve other gods before me." It does not say that you can't have other gods or spirits, so long as you put Almighty God first.

Michael, my older brother, was already going to residential school in Chesterfield Inlet when I really started to remember things. There is little I do not remember after he came home after his first year. It was about the same time that my father also came home from spending time at a sanatorium in Manitoba for tuberculosis. They both had amazing stories from the south. From his experience down there, my father told us about plugging wires or ropes into walls to make lights work, of record players, and of other implements. He also spoke of tokens people had in their pockets and that they could trade these tokens at any store. Michael told us of the language he was learning in school and one of the huge buildings he shared with many other Inuit of many different dialects. In this dawn of change, my younger brother and I were still just trying to figure out why the trader had brown stool and not black like the rest of us.

Ours was a strange world full of wonder. It seemed as if it could not get any better because we had everything a child could ever want. I was about seven years old and had a promised wife, whom I was very shy with, but I followed the rules and gave her everything from soap to oranges. We had many dogs, each with a name. We had freedom and rules to enjoy our freedom, and, as children, we were encouraged to be playful and have fun. We had a child's language, which we were to use until we became old enough to use a more mature Inuit language. We only heard innocent stories, as we were asked to go outside to play when the adults were discussing mature subjects. We had chores, such as getting water and training puppies. We observed as much as we were allowed to. There were rituals to keep us safe and keep us from sickness. Cyril and I were inseparable. We did everything together. We sometimes thought we were the only two people in the whole world.

Being Taken

Then one day a "flyable" took me away from our world through the sky to a dark and desolate place. I do not remember having time to say goodbye to Cyril, my soulmate. I do not remember saying goodbye to the puppies or the bright environment before we boarded the RCMP Single Otter to go to Chesterfield Inlet Residential School. I seem to remember playing with Cyril and then seeing the Union Jack put up the flagpole that signified a plane was going to come in, which was always a fun time. Perhaps, as always, the pilot would have a sucker for us, but this time the sucker was me. Michael was on the plane with me. He was my older brother, but he was not Cyril. Perhaps we were close at one time, but his time in residential school had alienated us somewhat. Still, because he was a sibling and of blood, I hung on to him. I did everything he did. When he looked out the window of the plane, I searched to see what he was looking at. When he closed his eyes, I did too, but opened mine often to see if he had opened his. I observed everything he did as I was taught to observe and do. I was on my own now, still a child with Inuit child language, not old enough to be on my own. But now, my childhood was behind me. I was on my own. I thought perhaps Judgment Day had come and we were going to a very happy place, but then again, the plane landed on the sea.

I remember fish swimming under the pontoons of the plane. I remember being carried by one of the pilots to the beach, whimpering and thinking we were going to be left behind. The pilots smiled and spoke gibberish to us, and, before sunset, we took off again to finish our trip, which I had hoped would never end. The unknown was numbing to think about.

Because time must elapse, it did, and too soon we landed in the dark on a lake somewhere. I do not know about the other children, but I was now following my brother and not focusing on anything else. He was all I had left. He probably talked to me, but the fear was overwhelming, so I tried not to see or focus on anything else. I would then hang on to my older brother for the rest of the trip. Everyone else and everything was black.

The School

Entering "the hostel," it was impossible to ignore all your senses. Strange voices and languages could be heard in the distance, strange new smells permeated the air at the doorway, and everything was painted in white, in contrast to the people in black. My brother and I were immediately separated, as we were seemingly separated by size. Now, I was alone, alone as I had never been before. A cry was in my throat, but being there with other children my size, it was not the right thing to do. I did not cry and did as little as possible so as not to attract attention from the Sisters (nuns). We were taken to the kitchen and mess hall and then given tea and "Roman Catholic" biscuits. In Repulse Bay, Roman Catholic biscuits were rare, so we always ate them slowly to see who would have the last enviable mouthful. But in my new world, "*Vite!*" ("Quickly!") was the word being repeated. One of the nuns would put her hand under the children's chins, making them chew faster and repeating this word, "*Vite, vite!*" From that moment on, *vite* became a normal word, as we were to do most things in a hurry. When we did not *vite*, we were half lifted by the ear and made to *vite*.

After tea and biscuits, I had to pee, but had no way of knowing how to ask and dared not attract more attention than necessary. I thought surely they would take us outside to pee, or maybe to a real toilet room like in the HBC staff house. Instead, we were led into the bedroom—the biggest room I had seen in my life up to that time—and told to undress and put on a new set of soapy-smelling clothes. The nun mumbled many meaningless things, but I kept my head down like the huskies we controlled, lest we yelled at them more. I eyed where they put my brother and, after what sounded like "Hail Mary," we were put to bed. The nun went to every bed and made sure that we all had our hands visible on top of the blankets (apparently, I later learned, so that we did not masturbate) and out went the lights. In Repulse Bay, I had shared a bed with my brother Cyril all my life, and now I was sharing with a room full of seemingly countless children who spoke, cried, walked, and tossed and turned. I tried not to move in case one of the sleepwalkers came my way, and then sometime during the night, I fell asleep looking towards my brother's way.

I remember dreaming, not of family or of home, but about this kid who we were told about during catechism. He was trying to empty the ocean with a spoon. The point, apparently, was that it was impossible. I remember always thinking it was possible. Anyhow, he put out his hand holding a thimble and told me to pee in it. I told him I should not, but he was so peaceful and innocent and he was in our catechism, so I relented and peed in the thimble, at first holding back so I did not overflow it. Then, when it did not overflow, I let out a flood. To my surprise, I relieved myself without ever filling the thimble. When he proceeded to carefully pour the thimble into the spoon, I woke up to the nun doing her wake-up call. I saw then that everyone was wearing the kind of clothing I was given the night before, and the nun was holding the same kind of clothing herself. She made folding motions, which everyone else was doing, so I folded my dripping-with-pee clothes and put them under my pillow as instructed. I followed others in the procedure of washing, brushing teeth, and breakfast, and then went to my first day of school.

The first morning of school was surprisingly nice, as the creatures of the night before were a distant memory now. We were even given hot chocolate, a rare drink in Repulse Bay, and then we took a nap. This is not so bad, I thought. The morning ended too fast, it seemed, when we had to go back to the hostel for lunch. At least that was what they told us. At the hostel doorway, our supervisor was waiting and nudging everyone as they went by her in single file. Since the morning went so well, I had my head up to observe what other children were doing so I could do the same. I stepped up to the nun and waited for a nudge, but instead of a nudge, I got pulled by the ear and, nearly hanging in the air, I hopped alongside her while willing myself not to cry.

We stopped next to my bed with the sheets pulled out. She made it obvious that she wanted me to carry them, so I did. I could hardly see over the sheets, blanket, and pyjamas in front of me, but I did not have to, as my ear was leading me to my next stop, a washing tub. I washed the sheets and pyjamas with a bar of soap and wrung them out as much as I could. The nun kept yelling gibberish to me throughout "lunchtime," and by the time I was finished, it was time to go back to school. I asked what my school friends had for lunch and was told frozen fish, biscuits, and tea. Frozen fish? In the summer? How do you freeze fish in the summer? Their answer was, "I do not know." School was fun, though. We learned many things we never knew existed. All the trees had apples or oranges. There were bears of different colours. We counted numbers that went beyond 20.

There was a Qallunaaq boy named Dick who had a funny-looking dog. Singing, art, and science were my favourite subjects. One day our teacher told us that plants grow because of water and that if we water plants we can help them grow. During recess I found fall flowers and watered them daily, and sure enough, they seemed to be growing. When freeze-up time came, I made a little snow shelter for them and continued to water them. Then one day a blizzard came and I could not find them anymore, but I thought about them throughout the year, and the following spring I found them again. The ice buildup had protected them.

They also taught us to play bingo. At my first bingo game I won cigarettes. I was so happy they asked me to give these to some older Inuk, and, later, a teacher gave me a skunk figurine. We also played "mass" with child-size chalices, tabernacle, robes, and so on. One evening, when we were playing mass, we heard this girl crying with all her might. Then we saw it was the oldest girl in the hostel, being dragged down the stairs by her long hair. She was holding her own hair with both hands so the nun would not pull it out by the roots. She was made to apologize for saying "bad things" to some boy. I felt some guilt, as she was the girl the oldest boy used to have me deliver messages to about where to meet.

I was the youngest child in the school at the time and getting picked on horribly by a gang of older children. Amongst other things, they would stick a knife into the snow with the blade up, and I was forced into a push-up position over the knife. They would then take turns stepping on my back. One day the oldest boy said he would protect me from anyone if I would take messages to the oldest girl, which I gladly did for the protection. He kept his word, and no one bothered me after that.

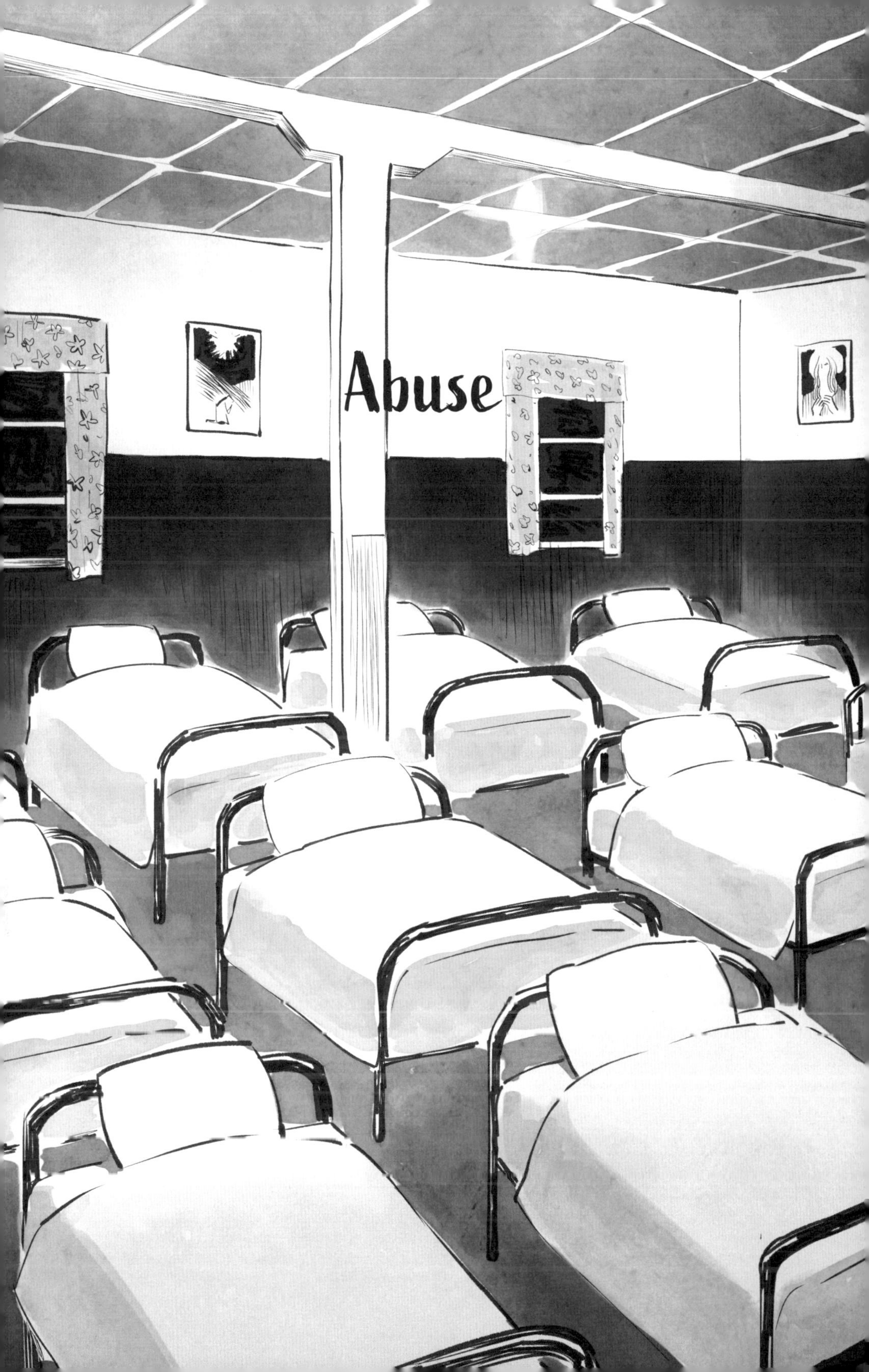
Abuse

One day I heard there was "abuse" at the school. It reminded me of my mother, who had spent time at a nun convent, telling us before we left for the residential school that we should never be touched on certain parts of our body. I guess she knew "things" about certain priests or brothers. Later on, her words served well for me and, apparently, my older brother, as many of the unfortunate victims were terribly sexually abused. (I only learned of this as an adult, after the residential schools issue started coming out.) These were some of the boys I went to school with, and they never shared any of this, as they were kept silent with threats. One of them told me they were made to sit side-by-side naked while they were waiting to be taken to the Brother's bed to service him one by one. When one was done, he would have to tell the next boy it was his turn, and so on.

Bad Times, Good Times

For all the horrible stories, there are as many or more happy stories: Christmas plays, feasts, letters from home, bishop visits, anointings, learning new things, coming of spring, last days of school, and going home. Bishop visits were particularly happy occasions. All the rooms were transformed with colourful, silky coverings—light pink, yellow, and purple. All the beds were covered with these magical covers. High Mass was done royally with all the priests in their finest, with canes, hats, and fine jewellery. The Gay Pride parade in Toronto would be jealous of this. As fast as the magic appeared, it disappeared when the bishop left. Everything was dark and gloomy once again.

When spring was coming, things seemed to ease, or perhaps our minds were preoccupied with thoughts of home. There were snowless patches of earth to play in, lemmings to kill, puddles to jump into, and punishments that did not seem to happen as often. The frozen fish, *maktaaq* (whale skin), caribou, and other meats were not so frozen at suppertime. Cleaning up classrooms and school things meant that the time of going home was coming soon. We just could not count the days, as we never knew until we were *vited* to the airplane.

Going Home

Going home after being away for 10 months brought thoughts of puppies, little sister, Mother and Father, and of course, Cyril. But the truth is that one can never really go home again. My family had grown more at home. Cyril had matured a year as an Inuk. His Inuit language had changed; his observations and doings were beyond mine as an Inuk. Yes, I had learned some foreign knowledge, but I had not aged at home. The puppies grew up, my sister was no longer a baby, and my parents acted differently towards me, as they were not quite sure how to address me or how I would react. My language and mannerisms were still so childish after a year of being away. But after some minor tweaking adjustments, Cyril and I had two months to be who we were and are: two free spirits with much to learn from each other. We laugh heartily because we now have brown stool, just like the white folk.

Year of the Apology

For many years I had argued within myself over the good and the bad of going to residential school. I always sided with the government and the churches, as I thought they were on the side of the angels. They were only following a curriculum that had no Inuit cultural content at all. They could only teach what they knew, and, of course, they could not teach what they did not know. I knew there were exercises where students were not allowed to speak their mother tongue, but in linguistic terms, this is known as a "full immersion" language course. I had not learned about hunting, skinning, and iglu building because I had not had the opportunity. I heard this assimilation was intentional, but it could have been done so smoothly that I did not know that it happened to me. I am observant because I am Inuk and smart enough to know that, as an Inuk, I am way behind students who quit school or never went. I know less than them about Inuit culture and language, but that goes with the territory.

I was asked by Inuit Tapiriit Kanatami to join Mary Simon in attending Prime Minister Harper's "offer of full apology on behalf of Canadians for the Indian Residential Schools system." Unfortunately, I was committed to going somewhere else, but on June 11, 2008, I listened to every word on CBC Radio: "The federal government, partly in order to meet its obligation to educate aboriginal children, began to play a role." That was why my mother blindly allowed us to be taken away year after year. The Prime Minister continued:

> *Two primary objectives of the residential school system were to remove and isolate children from the influence of their homes, families, traditions and cultures, and to assimilate them into the dominant culture. These objectives were based on the assumption aboriginal cultures and spiritual beliefs were inferior and unequal. Indeed, some sought, as it was infamously said, "to kill the Indian in the child."*

For some reason I missed my mother then. I was numb and had an uncontrollable urge to cry, but the residential school had taught me to keep my cry underground. I cry when I am alone. After *mamiattugut* (the apology) and "forging a new relationship between aboriginal peoples and other Canadians," I made a hard copy of the text and went to board my plane to deal with the Dene/Inuit Manitoba border issue.

Thank you to all who made this happen. You have achieved no less than Mahatma Gandhi and Martin Luther King Jr. achieved for their people. You have freed us through peace and persistence, and that includes you, Prime Minister.

Merci, thank you, *masi cho, qujannamiik!*

Remember, though, we are all accountable for things we do and for things we do not do.

About the Author

Jose Amaujaq Kusugak was born in 1950, in an iglu in Naujaat (then Repulse Bay), located on the Arctic Circle. Both of his parents had worked for the Hudson's Bay Company; his father was a handyman, and his mother worked as a cleaner and fur washer. Jose went to school in Chesterfield Inlet and Rankin Inlet, Nunavut, and Churchill, Manitoba. He attended high school in Saskatoon, Saskatchewan. After graduation, he returned to Nunavut to work at the Eskimo Language School, a branch of the University of Saskatchewan, in Kangiqłiniq (Rankin Inlet). Later, he taught Inuktitut and Inuit history at Churchill Vocational Centre.

Jose became active in Inuit politics in 1971, shortly after the founding of the Inuit Tapiriit Kanatami (ITK) (then Inuit Tapirisat of Canada). He persuaded the new organization of the critical need to standardize the written Inuit language, which is primarily an oral language. However, funding for this project had been delayed, so Jose worked as an assistant to Tagak Curley, the founder of ITK, and introduced the concept of land claims to Inuit in the Arctic. In 1974, he went to Alaska to study how the land claims process worked there. From 1980 to 1990, Jose worked as the area manager of CBC in the Kivalliq region. He served as president of Nunavut Tunngavik Incorporated, one of four regional organizations that make up ITK, from 1994 to 2000. He was elected president of ITK in June 2000. He described the relationship of the Inuit to Canada as "First Canadians, Canadians First."

Jose Kusugak died in 2011 in Kangiqłiniq.